Togetherness

Healthy Friendships,

Relationships,

and Communities

Also by Teresa Griffith

Love Your Skeletons
York Boat Captain—18 Life-Changing Days on the
Peace River
Forging Sisterhood in the Frozen North

In the **Tiny Books on Big Ideas** series:
It All Belongs — The Law of Attraction and Nature
of the Universe
Intelligence is Everywhere — Looking at Animals,
Vegetables, and Minerals
Two Trees — Attitudes that Lead to Wellness

Togetherness

Healthy Friendships,

Relationships,

and Communities

Teresa Griffith

Tiny Books on Big Ideas - Book 4

Cover design and typography by Teresa Griffith
Available for print-on-demand by Lulu.com

teresagriffith.ca

ISBN 978-0-9921204-4-3

In gratitude and appreciation

for my sweet and amazing

husband, Darren

Contents

Acknowledgements

You may have heard that writing a book is a labour of love. While it may be labour for some, for me, it is play. I am happiest when I am indulging in one of my creative outlets and I love to write, so the greater hardship would be keeping all these ideas in. It does take time, however, and many tasks such as yard work, weeding the garden and doing the dishes did suffer while I focused on finishing these tiny books. For his patience, literary suggestions, editing skill and most of all, his unbelievable love, I must thank my husband, Darren Griffith. He is so dear to me, and I know that this series would not have been as easy without his help, nor would the quality of the finished product be as high.

I must extend special thanks to all my lovely friends in Edmonton and sprinkled around Alberta. Thank you so much for all your encouragement, smiles, hugs and acceptance. I love you all!

Two friends I met when I lived up north have been invaluable in giving feedback and suggestions to the final draft. Michelle Clarke, thank you for everything. There is no doubt in my mind that these tiny books are better thanks to you. I would love to thank Tim Brown for all the deep conversations. To all my many other northern friends, I appreciate and love you more than you know!

Lastly, I must acknowledge my phenomenal family. I am who I am in large part because of the foundation you gave me. You continue to shower me with love and acceptance, along with practical help and good advice. My dad, Rudy Kneller, my mom, Donna Kneller and my sisters, Patricia and Gina, I love you and appreciate you so much.

Successful marriage is leading innovative lives together, being open, non-programmed. It's a free fall: how you handle each new thing as it comes along. As a drop of oil on the sea, you must float, using intellect and compassion to ride the waves.

- Joseph Campbell

Introduction

Birds of a feather flock together.

It was the first warmish day of spring. The sun had finally broken through the low cloud and was shining and warming the air up nicely. Living on a small farm as I do, I went to sit out on a small pile of hay bales to bask—fully-clothed—in the sun. This is what Canadians do on the first warmish day of spring when it's still too cold for tanning. We sit in the sun wearing black and get some sun on our faces and hands, and maybe arms!

Since it was the first warmish day, the birds were also out enjoying it, and many had just arrived back from their winter migrations. I heard a few sporadic bird songs, from all directions, and mostly in the distance. I quickly gave up trying to identify them all—I am no expert in bird songs—but I did think I heard something from the sandpiper family from the direction of the low-lying grasslands on the edge of our land. I noticed one small black bird with a very pretty song sitting on a power line nearby, and then an enormous flock of more small black birds flew into the spruce trees that form the southern wind break. There were probably a hundred of them! I wondered why the black bird on the wire did not join the others.

It must not be the same species, I concluded, although the calls sounded similar to my amateur ears. If it was the same species, it would *certainly* be in the flock—I have never seen a flocking bird sitting away from the others, by itself. It just doesn't happen. You may see one completely on its own—like the single Canada goose I saw the other day flying overhead—but if there are others of its kind around, a stray will join a flock. It's instinct for them, the same way sheep or alpacas like to be in a herd. In a flock of birds, you'll rarely see an oddball of another species either—I guess that's how the expression "birds of a feather flock together" came to be.

That expression is usually used to say that people tend to hang out with people who are like them (a good piece of evidence for the Law of Attraction, if you still need more). So, are people like birds? Are we meant to live in a flock? Or are we meant to live more as grizzly bears, in solitude that is only interrupted for the purpose of mating and raising young?

I think in general, we are meant to live in community. Think of a cave man; he had a better standard of living when he was in a village than hunting on his own. Different members of the village could do different tasks—scraping hides, watching children, and sharpening spears. Together they could accomplish more, and be happier doing it, and the same is still true today.

Sitting on the hay bales, I noticed the huge flock in the spruce trees suddenly erupt in a chorus of cheeping and flying. They weren't singing—those birds sounded agitated! Maybe someone in the flock landed on someone else—it's got to happen occasionally—and so the victim lashed out and 99 others joined in. The same happens with people. We *can* be happier living in community, but only until someone is upset with someone else and lashes out, talks behind their back, or won't forgive. This can make us want to live as a grizzly bear, completely on our own, but if we can learn to navigate these difficulties, we will be happier in some kind of community.

So, living in relationships, in community, is necessary, yet it's not something we are officially taught. We learn it "on the street" and on the playground, but our instructors are generally our peers—and can be as inept as we are at relating. Although the opening quote from Joseph Campbell is about marriage, this tiny book will take a look at lots of different ways we relate—as acquaintances, friends and in love. We'll explore ways we can improve on teamwork, essential attitudes for harmonious relationships, and perhaps even try to understand how to live peacefully with a mate!

As with the other tiny books, take your time reading through the chapters one at a time. You may find the principles that follow will stretch your brain, beliefs and understanding of how relationships work.

Togetherness

The Flip Side of the Golden Rule

Do unto others
as you would have them do unto you.

I love to look at common knowledge, sayings or tidbits of wisdom and see if there is more to them. You have probably heard The Golden Rule—do unto others as you would have them do unto you. There is a profound and universal truth to another whole aspect— the flip side—of this saying:

What someone does to you,
they are doing to themselves.

When someone is unkind, it's because they are unhappy with themselves. When someone is angry at you, they are angry at themselves. When they hurt you, it's because they want to hurt themselves.

The opposite is also true:

What you do to another,
you do to yourself.

When you are kind to someone else, you are showing kindness to yourself. When you are compassionate, you are showing compassion to yourself. When you give someone a hug or even a simple pat on the arm, you are treating yourself to the experience of giving them comfort or joy.

I know it might be a stretch for you, but please stay with me. This is profound. Think about how you feel when you speak to another nicely, and how you feel when you are sharp. Last time you got mad at someone, could it be you were actually mad at yourself? When you are feeling good about yourself, isn't it a hundred times easier to do something nice for someone else? Sure, we can force ourselves to be considerate, but it's not the same. What we do to another, we do to ourselves, because we are all one.

I have found when I am able to love the ones who have hurt me, I am loving myself in the deepest, most profound way possible. When I forgive those who wronged me, I am being forgiving—being compassionate, dwelling in the place of forgiveness—with myself. If I refuse to do these things, I am essentially refusing to accept that *I* am worthy of love, worthy of respect, worthy as a human being.

Realize that if you won't forgive another, you are only holding yourself back. If you refuse to love, you are only closing *yourself* up to all the Love that could come your way, if you allowed it. Although you might have a pattern of being unloving toward yourself, why not make a change? Dare to like yourself. Dare to think that you're okay! Dare to be understanding instead of judgmental towards yourself. You are awesome, and you're on a journey of growth that can be uncomfortable at times—growing pains, perhaps—but it's also a journey of heart and I promise you, there is *pure love and joy* at the end.

~

This flip side of the golden rule is why it's so important to be aware of how you are feeling about/towards yourself. It is why we need quiet and contemplation time to gain some measure of awareness of our own state to be able to identify how our own feelings are contributing to the situation at hand. In terms of vibration, the thoughts I am thinking about myself determine my vibration and what kinds of experiences I am attracting (see Tiny

Book 1 *It All Belongs - The Law of Attraction and Nature of the Universe* for more on this).

Let's look at an example. I might get mad at someone—let's call him Mike—because I'm still mad about something unrelated that happened this morning. I might be mad about not having time for breakfast but I'm really mad at myself for not getting out of bed sooner. I hate not having enough time in the morning. Meanwhile poor Mike has no idea why I'm peeved at him over something so small. I *seem* mad at him, but I'm really mad at myself.

Often, the situation is more convoluted, and the reason I'm mad at myself is not related to missing breakfast. Sometimes when running errands, I get annoyed at my husband but the root of the issue is that I'm not leaving any margin in my life—I'm filling every available minute with a task, errand, or phone call. I might even blame *him* for not having any margin in *my life,* but that is obviously me trying to avoid taking responsibility for my life. I could plan my time better. I could live simpler and have fewer errands overall. My frustration may in fact stem from the dissonance in saying I want a simpler life and then buying or doing things that make it more complicated. Have you noticed that more gadgets means less simplicity? So, the true cause of the annoyance or anger is very different from the surface cause.

Kindness, compassion, understanding and tolerance of others are only possible when you display these attitudes and feelings towards yourself. Meditate on one of these words and turn the word-feeling inward towards yourself. Accept love and understanding from Source.

Unconnected

When I lived in Wrigley, Northwest Territories, Canada, for a month I had no home phone, internet or TV. Perhaps you think I barely survived, but in fact, it was enjoyable and I learned a lot from the experience of being unconnected to the rest of the world.

I was working every day, so I had use of the phone to make any calls I needed to. The internet there was dial-up, and was set up for a specific sending procedure, so I couldn't go online at work at all (I tried going to the Google homepage and it wouldn't even begin to load). Since I had no connectivity at home— I forgot to mention, there was no cell service either—when I left work for the day, I was leaving a lot behind.

Off and on, I dealt with bouts of anger and frustration at not having my phone hooked up yet. The one and only phone company that served that area was appalling. With no competition, they had really let their customer service slide. Their delays and excuses were astounding. I eventually decided that I wasn't going to be mad about it any more. Everything else about my life was great and I didn't want to let that one thing mess up the rest. From that point on, I started to feel happier and more at ease.

The atmosphere at my unconnected place was interesting. Pleasant. Peaceful. There were no interruptions and no outside influences that my roommate and I didn't specifically invite in. We listened to the radio a fair bit; there were only two stations up there, and we usually tuned in to CBC North. We also listened to music, and enjoyed introducing each other to our favourite artists and songs. We had both played in bands of our own in the past, and it was fun to relate our experiences with music and performing. One night, we sat for a couple of hours on the couch, relaxed, just chatting about music. There was no TV to invade our intentions, no internet to distract us or phones to demand our attention. Sure, there were lots of times every day that I wished I could look something up online, and there were a few websites I missed visiting.

I thought I would miss connecting with my family and friends more, but I found that although **we all need connection**, it doesn't have to be with who we think. I was completely happy connecting with my roommie, who I had just met, and I also made some new and unlikely friends there who I connected with, too. Through making eye contact, shaking hands or hugging, we had real conversations and a real connection. Having all the technology in the world doesn't help us connect; it *can* help, but it can also be a huge distraction. Most tech is meant to help us connect over long distances, but we desperately need in-person connections, too. Without them, we wither and feel depressed.

Keep in mind, I am a natural introvert—I am not someone who "needs people," yet I have found that I do. I thrived so much more with my roommate in Wrigley than when I went there the previous spring and didn't see a single soul outside of my work hours. I didn't have any tech connectivity then either, so I was completely alone after 4:30 pm each day. For safety reasons, I sent an "I'm okay" message using a GPS device—one-way communication—to my boss and my husband each night and morning. Although I was okay, I wasn't exactly thriving. Luckily, I was only there for two weeks—I'm not sure what the long-term results of that experiment in isolation would have been.

I wonder how different the world would be if everyone made one non-friend connection each day. It could be chatting with a stranger on the bus, making eye contact with another person in line at the grocery store, or smiling at an acquaintance for no reason. We might become less dependent on our spouses and closest friends to provide our every need when it comes to connection. We must not fall into the trap of thinking that connecting with our loved ones makes us happy; we *individually* make ourselves happy. It's not up to anyone else—or technology—to do it for us.

It Takes One to Know One

I met a man recently who liked to rant about how a coworker of his was such a bully. Of course, he was the hero in the story he was telling, standing up to the bully, calling him out on it, and not letting the man push him around. The result was two strong-headed people pushing against each other, a fair bit of name-calling, and before long, they no longer had to work together. The "hero" of the story got fired from the job.

I couldn't help but think it takes one to know one. The man who was so adamant and upset about the bully was clearly a bit of one himself. Bullying is strange that way—and we've been seeing more of it in our schools for a few reasons.

First, because we look for it and label it.

The more you look for something, the more you will find it.

Second, because adults do a lot of bullying. Our children are learning it from us. They see people driving aggressively and yelling and screaming at car accident scenes. They overhear people bad-talking the opposing sports team, using violent, angry words. The news is full of stories of people bullying others all the time, whether it is cops, individuals, politicians or armies. Kids also see principals bully teachers, or teachers bullying each other.

It's interesting, though, that I have no bullies in my life. I cannot think of anyone—acquaintance or co-worker, friend or neighbour—who I feel is a bully. Why is that? Perhaps it is because I don't have a bullying vibe at all, so I neither see nor attract those people. Maybe one of my neighbours is a bully —but how would I know if I never have those sorts of interactions with him? If I don't push him around, he won't push me. The only time in recent memory I felt like I was being pushed around was by a small, spunky beagle I was dog-sitting. That dog would do *anything* to go for a walk!

So how do we stop the bullying in the world around us? It's simple, but not quick. We have to be more peaceful. We have to have more gratitude for and focus on the good things around us. We have to be more accepting of others, and ourselves. We have to respect others deeply. We have to live and let live. We have to choose the non-violent solution *every time.* We have to resist the urge to raise our voice. We have to look away from anger. We have to let feelings of frustration pass through us without acting on them. We have to find a way to address an angry person with calmness and openness.

We have to tap into a deeper source of inner peace and acceptance. Easier said than done, when we are surrounded by the troubles and busyness of the modern world. We must rise above people mistreating each other. We must choose to focus on the lovely things of the world, see beauty everywhere and give our best attention to what we want more of — peaceful, positive, uplifting interactions with others, respectful relationships, and happy experiences.

It really does take one to know one. We must become what we want to know and see more of. As Gandhi said, we must be the change we want to see in the world. We must see and focus upon whatever we want to be.

Solitude and Togetherness

I am naturally quite adventurous and one year, I did a seven-day kayaking trip all by myself. I was writing a paddling guide for a river, and I didn't have anyone to go with me, so I went on my own. I had a GPS tracker and locator device, so I could call for help in an emergency, but I was otherwise completely on my own and self-sufficient.

I was pretty nervous for the first few days. Anything could go wrong! I could lose my paddle... and my spare paddle! I could capsize near the shore and lose all my gear. I could get separated from my boat and be stranded on an island! I had to be careful. By the fourth day, I was able to relax a bit and enjoy the experience more. On the fifth day, I woke up with very sore shoulders—I had been pushing myself every day to go farther and it was starting to take its toll. I had to be much more mindful of every stroke and use my back and torso muscles more, to save my shoulders. Part way through the sixth day, I had to go ashore and wait out a huge thunderstorm—on the river bank, with no shelter at all. I thought it might be the end of me! I got absolutely soaked, but was not struck by lightning. When the storm was over, I went a little farther and camped on a large, flat clearing along the river bank, near a small house. The owner came by later and we had a lovely time around the campfire, talking about the river, society and life. At the end of the trip, I was exhilarated, vibrant, strong, and more independent than ever. I had not looked in a mirror for seven days, and I saw myself as a gorgeous, sun-bleached blonde, tanned goddess!

The ride home was also a trip off cloud nine. My husband was stressed about something—I had no idea what. I couldn't look out the window while he drove—it was too fast. I had not travelled faster than 15 km/h for days and highway speed was too much for me. I could not bear to be indoors. The sky was my roof and the house seemed *far* too small. Then I got a glimpse of myself in a mirror—I was not the blonde goddess I had envisioned.

I had to redefine myself, again. I had to adjust to living with others, and navigating society. It might have only been seven days, but a lot happened on that trip.

The next year, I was part of a group that built a large wooden York boat to row and sail the same river for 18 days in a historical reenactment. It was a very different experience because I was not alone. I had my crew. I was in charge, and they were the best crew I could have hoped for. They were helpful and hardworking, with positive attitudes and good senses of humour. We accomplished our voyage safely and successfully because we worked together so well. It was another life-changing experience, and I wrote a memoir of it to share what an incredible experience it was. (It is called *York Boat Captain - 18 Life-Changing Days on the Peace River.*)

So you see, I've had experiences of solitude so deep and teamwork so complete, I've seen the whole spectrum of togetherness. I learned some things from my solo trip that I would never learn in a group, including defining myself with no one else's input or judgment. It gave me renewed confidence and profound self-acceptance. I had only my thoughts as company, and they evolved from worry and busyness, to quiet observation of my surroundings and mindfulness, to deep appreciation and serenity. There are definitely things to be learned from time spent alone, and the more time in solitude, the deeper one can go.

Yet none of us can live in solitude on the long term. To accomplish the greatest things, we need to work with others. On the York boat, we experienced a lovely sense of camaraderie, family and oneness. We had a goal to work towards, and we did so with respect, thoughtfulness, helping one another and enjoying each other's company. We also had a lot of fun! My definition of myself blurred into identification with my crew; we became a single unit. Four of us were together for nearly every minute of 18 days; a few other people filled in spots on the crew for shorter periods, but at the end of the trip, those of us in the core group hardly knew how to be apart. I felt very strange when separated from them, as if part of my body were missing.

There is such beautiful potential for cooperation and collaboration when we work together. It is worth striving for. Living peacefully in community is one of the noblest goals—and is as fulfilling as watching one's child grow up. Like so many things, it works better when we do it whole-heartedly. A group where people help each other often, share their struggles and victories, and would do anything for each other is a true community. Neighbours can work on projects together or watch each other's kids (or pets). Coworkers can genuinely try to make each other's work go smoothly, to cooperate and communicate for the better accomplishment of their tasks and a more harmonious workplace.

The people of Denmark created a way of living together called **co-housing** that allows people to live in community. While every family or individual has their own private space, the co-housing building or yard has common areas such as a kitchen, dining room, playgrounds, workshops or fitness rooms, depending on what their members want. Everyone eats together regularly and helps each other with things like childcare, gardening and maintenance projects. Co-housing creates a village in a city where co-housers know their neighbours and have a feeling of community and togetherness that is missing in much of our modern society, and it's becoming popular around the world.

~

There are two roadblocks to healthy communities and workplaces I'd like to mention. The first is villainizing. We must stop ourselves as soon as we start to think of someone as bad. Villainizing starts easily; if someone is momentarily inconsiderate or critical of us, we can quickly start labeling them with all sorts of colourful adjectives. We tell ourselves a story about what a jerk they are; we make them into a villain in our heads. Alternatively, when someone is simply different and we don't understand their actions or motives, we are tempted to judge, label and villainize. Without realizing it, this handicaps our interactions with them in the future; it is much harder to be open-minded and clear-thinking because we can't forget the fictional story we told ourselves about them. Villainizing starts in our heads and leads to the second obstacle to loving communities: gossip. Speaking in unkind words about each other *fractures our souls.* Being mean to a teammate, family member or coworker is harmful *to us.* We have to stop gossip before it leaves our lips. I find by ignoring any gossip around me, it does not spread and I don't give my energy to it or to the gossipers. I talk *to* people, not *about* people. In some situations, the leader of a group may need to speak to a gossiper and discourage them from their hobby. In all cases, the leader sets the tone for the group, so when I have that privilege, I am careful about how I conduct myself. I look for ways to help the people I'm leading flourish.

In many ways, we're all leaders. There are a hundred small ways to make a community out of the people around you, but it won't work as well if you don't know yourself. Keep solitude and togetherness in balance. Any time you need to, spend some time alone in nature to reset your self-image and recharge your soul. Get to know what your common thought patterns are. Write in a journal if that works for you. Know your own buttons—what makes you mad—and acknowledge the hurts you've endured. Appreciate the uniqueness that is you, and don't let any view in the mirror get in the way of that.

Energy Shifts

You are not who you think you are—no one is. With no distractions, when you are truly alone with yourself, who are you?

How can you find this out? Be alone. When I went on my big kayaking trip, I started to feel like I was truly being myself on the fourth day. Something in me shifted. I became... genuine. I stopped a charade I didn't even know I'd been playing, and dropped all pretenses. Why would I have pretenses with myself? I don't know. All I know is that I felt an energy shift. Try spending at least three or four days completely alone, with no outside contact of any kind, in nature. You'll get closer to meeting your true self.

Why bother? Why meet yourself? An interesting thing happens when you spend time by yourself—when you really connect with yourself and your intuition—and then reestablish contact with those closest to you (boy/girlfriend, husband/wife, best friend, etc). At the moment you see him/her, you will feel another shift. This time it is the shift that occurs when you put the persona or pretenses back on, and when you do so, if you pay attention, you can learn a great deal about yourself and your relationships.

I've noticed that I feel different every time my husband and I are apart for several days. I can, once again, tell that a pretense has fallen away. It's a good feeling! I feel comfortable when Darren is around, yet when I am alone, I feel *totally at ease* in a different way. I have plenty of insight about why this is, but I don't want to share it and taint whatever insight you might get into *your* relationships.

Ideally, the energy shift you feel when you reunite is positive. If it isn't, there is no one to blame; there are simply things for you to learn about yourself and your relationship.

I realize that you might find it hard to take three or four days away to perform this experiment. You can try a shorter period of time—two days apart might be enough to feel the shift of "putting the mask back on." You don't have to go out into the wilderness as I did, but getting away from your usual scene would be helpful—going on a trip, even if it isn't very far away—and spending as much time in nature as possible, unplugged. Then, be *very alert* to how you feel when you reconnect with your significant other.

Can you sense how your partner sees you? Do you feel judged or labeled? Do you feel like you have to act a certain way? How far away from your authentic self does it feel? Do you think you can keep up the charade indefinitely? What do you think will happen if your facade fails? What will he/she think of you then? Are you afraid of losing your pretenses? Why? Please understand that I'm not saying there shouldn't be any masks or pretenses at all—having a "persona" or mask is not unusual or necessarily wrong—just think about what yours is and if you are prepared to wear it a lot, or if it is a very big stretch from your natural personality.

One-on-One Relationships

When I was in my twenties, I was very self-conscious about my large forehead. I felt it was so big, I grew bangs to cover it. And then one day, my friend Stacey heard me say something about it, and she told me that in art class, she learned that the forehead should take up half the face. She said to draw an oval for the head, and put the eyes in the middle, with equal space for the forehead and the rest of the face. This simple realization rocked my view of myself! I no longer had to hide my forehead. It was perfectly proportional to my face. I never worried about the size of my forehead again.

What if Stacey had not told me about forehead/face proportions? I might still be self-conscious and growing my bangs long if she had not offered her perspective.

This is the beauty of a close friendship. Friends share their perspective, helping us see that the struggles we're experiencing are normal, and reminding us that we're doing fine. At a deeper level, **we see ourselves through the eyes of another when we are one-on-one with them.**

Does this still apply for a non-friend? What if they are an angry spouse?

This sharing of perspectives is why it feels so awful to argue with our partner. We are compounding miscommunication, our need to be right, and unmet expectations with the angry viewpoint. We no longer get to see ourselves as good or lovely in his/her eyes; we see the anger and we can't help but take it personally. Don't forget—another person's anger is not simply about you. They are also angry at themselves and may be "transmitting angry" in all directions.

The tricky part is knowing what to

"own"—what anger is a result of something inconsiderate or hurtful that I did, or a result of my own messy vibration—and what to disown—anger that is more about the other person's internal state. It is never as simplistic as that, but rather a combination of some parts to own and other parts to disown.

~

I find it very uncomfortable when someone is angry at me. I'd much rather see love in their eyes. Well, the opposite is also true for others; they would much rather see love in MY eyes when they look at me.

Our eyes give away our thoughts—judgmental, angry, uncomfortable or whatever else. We can help an angry person by looking at them with love. Remember who they are when they are at their best. Remember that they are angry at themselves, and struggling. I have learned, slowly, that when my husband is upset about something—angry or depressed—**my judgment is not needed here; my love is.**

Sometimes, a friend, spouse, or relationship changes and we no longer find it possible to look at them with love. If we feel this way consistently, we need to examine ourselves for resentment or contempt - directed outward or inward. These attitudes kill relationships and also our health. Counseling may be helpful to get to the root of these emotions and diffuse them.

The strongest resentment/contempt I've seen is in abusive relationships. When someone is abusive, it is *necessary* to leave rather than try to love them whole again. Their issues are greater than any partner can repair. It is more important for you to be safe and take care of yourself if the friend/spouse is too angry. If their angry vibrations go out in all directions too strongly, the only way to interact with them will be in anger—through the Law of Attraction, they are drawing angry people to themselves. If you do not want to be an angry person, then you will naturally be non-attracted—repelled, one might say—from the relationship. If you stubbornly stay, two things will happen: it will no longer be a partnership, and you will become as angry as the abuser (although your anger may appear as fear or depression). To be happy, there is no other option but to leave an abuser and never go back.

~

To be in close relationship with another is like mixing paint, like a yin-yang symbol. We swirl around each other, have elements of each other inside us, and we see each other in unique ways.

We add our perspective to another, and we have the power to encourage and lift someone up—such as Stacey who set me straight about foreheads—or put someone down. Always choose life and love instead of being judgmental; whenever possible, choose to believe the best and look at them with love.

Growing a Love Garden

"At the end of the day people won't remember what you said or did, they will remember how you made them feel." - Maya Angelou

Suppose you meet someone special and before you know it, you fall in love. The two of you spend so much time together, you soon decide you want to grow a love garden together.

Everyone knows the analogies; to grow something in your life, you must prepare the soil, plant the seed and tend the garden. Let's explore those simple steps when it comes to romantic relationships.

"Preparing the soil" means making sure that you as an individual feel whole and complete on your own. If you are looking for someone to complete you, you will just attract someone by your flaws, feelings of brokenness or loneliness. You must have a hearty measure of self-

---

When you give your fullest attention to whoever you are interacting with, you take past and future out of the relationship, except for practical matters. When you are fully present with everyone you meet, you relinquish the conceptual identity you made for them— your interpretation of who they are and what they did in the past—and are able to interact without the egoic movements of desire and fear. Attention, which is alert stillness, is the key.

How wonderful to go beyond wanting and fearing in your relationships. Love does not want or fear anything.

- Eckhart Tolle in *Stillness Speaks*

---

love and self-assurance. Although no one is this way one hundred percent, the more whole you feel as a single person, the better.

Part of preparing the soil in your heart is dealing with your previous relationship and giving yourself some time in between. I'm sure you know the danger of rebounding; your old vibe is still going strong, so you are destined to repeat the same mistakes—with a new person, so it will *seem* different at first. When I was young and dating, I set aside a "recovery time" of half the length of the relationship that was ending. If I had dated a guy for a year, I planned to be single for six months afterwards in order to make sure I had plenty of time to think about what happened and deal with any baggage. This rule of thumb seemed to work well.

Then you must plant the seed. This equates to starting the new relationship, and frankly, this part takes care of itself. It will probably start out with a blaze of fireworks.

There is so much intense emotion in those early days! The world is beautiful, and our new love interest is so very interesting—they are flawless in our eyes. That's how it always is in the fresh blush of love. I'm not sure what is more exciting—thinking about our new boy/girlfriend, or thinking about how they like us too! We see ourselves through their eyes—"he likes me! He likes me! I guess I am pretty/handsome/ sexy/interesting/cool after all!"—and our mutual interest creates a new-love-feedback-loop that is so empowering and thrilling, it can be positively addictive. It is, in fact, for some people and that is why they never stick with one person for very long.

Once the seed is planted, you need to give it some time to sprout, so have patience. A new relationship will need time to grow as well. You need to get to know your sweetheart really well, and see what kind of love garden you can grow with them.

When the time is right, you may decide

this person is truly wonderful and you really want to move in together and/or get married and create a life together. Moving in together is a big step, not to be trivialized by saying it's just to save on rent or other mundane ways you may frame it. Living in the same place is a major milestone in a relationship and this is when the weeding starts.

No one talks about weeding the garden when they use the quaint planting seeds analogy. Make no mistake—weeding is essential! In my garden, the weeds grow like blockbusters, and if I don't keep pulling them, my poor vegetables or flowers don't have a chance. Any fertilizer I use just makes it worse! In long-term serious relationships, weeding is one of the most important factors.

Weeds are those tiny, inconsiderate, hurtful things we sometimes do, and they culminate in the worst weed of all—resentment. If we allow tiny bits of resentment or bitterness into our relationships—it does not matter what the cause is—we are essentially allowing thistles to grow wild in our love garden. In my main relationships, I guard against it. If I am upset about something, I talk it out and deal with it right away. I do not allow it to fester or simmer. I write in my journal to process things internally and look at my own behaviour and feelings. If I feel like I have missed an opportunity because of a relationship, I explore why I feel that way. I will never blame another for not letting me do something. I remind myself often that I am responsible for the direction of my life, so there is no place for blaming another for anything.

~

We must love ourselves to the core, to the best of our ability, and take care of our own happiness so that we don't do those tiny, hurtful things to our loved ones. Sarcastic comments, criticisms or secret judgments are all weeds in what is supposed to be our love garden. We may try to control the other person, or look down on them for something silly they've done. Unkind words are stinging nettle and like that spreading weed, they burn long after they are said.

To grow a healthy love garden, you have to watch out for these weeds in your own behaviour, without becoming too self-critical or perfectionistic. Be aware of them when they happen and stop them. Apologize. A simple, quick, "I'm sorry. I didn't mean to say that" can dull the sting of thoughtless words. Examining your behaviour and developing self-discipline is balanced with healthy self-love so that you don't get too critical or obsessed.

Besides weeding, there is watering and eventually picking the harvest. In our love garden, these equate to tending the relationship, caring for and showing gratitude and appreciation for the one you love. That new-love glow will wear off—that's a certainty —but your appreciation can continue to grow. It all depends on where you put your focus. You can decide to appreciate and amplify your loved one's strong points. Look at your partner with love.

Just because a relationship has been going on a long time doesn't mean you don't need to be nice. It's always important to watch out for the weeds of unkindness.

~

If you are looking for someone to start a relationship with, keep preparing your own soil and learning how to be a good partner. You can practice on your circle of friends— being kind, uplifting, and avoiding sarcasm, criticism and thoughtless words. You may be dealing with a lot of baggage from past relationships, but don't forget to cultivate self-love at the same time. By preparing your soil, when you do find someone interesting, you'll be ready for him/her to come alongside for a beautiful, healthy relationship.

Choosing to grow love and not weeds is simple. Removing the weeds from a relationship takes some work, but keeping it weed-free is easier than you think! The fruit you will pick will be sweet and lovely experiences in life.

Giving Advice

"If you can't say something nice,
don't say nothing at all."
- Thumper, from Bambi

The interesting thing about living in close proximity to someone is that you have a unique perspective on that person. Sometimes, it seems so clear what that person should do to improve their life or be happier, you want to tell them.

When you give advice, you are trying to do the job of your friend's or mate's intuition. If they listen to you, they won't be listening to their own inner guidance—they might even forget to check in with their intuition. Who do you think would do a better job of guiding them, you or their own intuition? Even if your intentions are good, you take second place to their intuition every time.

What if your intentions are not so good? It's pretty hard to have pure, selfless intentions all the time. You may be very tempted to give advice that will make them *and you* happier. It takes real maturity not to manipulate someone for your own purposes—not even a little.

So, it's best to avoid asking your partner to change something they're doing. No suggesting or hinting either! It's not your job to parent or control them. If you'd like them to change something minor and practical, then it can be done with kindness and a feeling of teamwork, such as "let's work together on keeping up with the dishes. If you load the dishwasher at night, I'll empty it in the morning." That's pretty straightforward. In most cases, however, **you have no right to ask your partner to change something about**

themselves. Let me gently ask: why are you with them if you don't like them as a person? Perhaps you actually don't like yourself lately?

If you notice your partner is changing, you may very mindfully and gently speak to him/her about it, but you must be prepared to address the same issue in yourself, too. Whenever you analyze your mate's behaviour, look at your own as well. You're co-creating now. As much as possible, be kind and non-judgmental of both of you.

~

People sometimes ask their partner to change or do something that they know he/she can't do. They set their mate up for failure on purpose and then when he/she fails, they have a way out that makes them feel good about themselves. They might say, "I told you what I needed, and you wouldn't do it, so I'm out of here!" If you catch yourself in this situation—tempted to ask for a change you are pretty sure your partner can't do—stop yourself and do some serious thinking about what has gone awry in your relationship. Why do you want to see them fail? Why do you feel so poorly about yourself? You're a beam of God-light; stop acting like you aren't.

Sometimes, the *demand* that someone change has an "or else" lingering in the air. If you're at the stage where you feel like saying "change or else I'll leave," then it is probably time to leave. It is definitely time to assess why you think you need that person to change and what attitude is making *you* so unhappy (read Tiny Book 3, *Two Trees - Attitudes That Lead to Wellness*).

Happiness is an inside job. No one else can make you happy. If you're unhappy, it's your own doing. If your relationship is completely sour or the two of you have grown apart, you have a decision to make, but do not blame anyone else for the situation you are in.

Often, feelings of unhappiness with someone have nothing to do with who they are (or who you are). You're unhappy because of the types of thoughts you have been thinking about them. **When you are judgmental or critical for any reason, you *will* feel unhappy** because you are so far out of alignment with the universe. The way of the universe is acceptance and growth, love and beauty. When you're critical, you're not in harmony with the universe, and your intuition sends you a signal—that feeling of unhappiness—to try to make you realize that. Criticizing anyone or anything will squash your happiness, and it's the **act of criticizing** that does it, not what anyone did. That's why accepting others feels so good—it is the opposite of criticizing and is in harmony with Spirit.

~

Stop judging, stop analyzing, and stop

criticizing. Start living in the moment, accepting who is around you. After all, your partner and close friends need your acceptance and love, not your advice.

Does Compatibility Matter?

They were like two peas in a pod.

When I was a young adult, I thought I could live with anyone. I am pretty easy-going, and I used to think that compatibility really wasn't all that important—if we loved each other, we would figure out a way to make it work.

In some ways, that seems a bit simplistic and naive, but in other ways, it is true. It's simplistic in the same way that I often forget that other people don't think like I do. We are all wired differently, and were raised differently, which means it's a rare thing to find someone who approaches challenges the same way I do. While it is possible for me to be happy with someone very different from myself, we would both need to be *exceptionally mature and have a great deal of love.*

Let's look at these concepts. What do I mean when I say "exceptionally mature?" We would need to be very accepting and non-judgmental. We would need to refrain from giving advice and never demand that our partner change. We would need to choose the tree of life and never choose the tree of criticism (see Tiny Book 3 *Two Trees - Attitudes That Lead to Wellness* for more on that). We would have to give up our desire/need to be right. We wouldn't compete with each other or play games for affection or approval.

What do I mean when I say "have a great deal of love?" I mean that we are tapped into the well of Universal Love. We love and are happy with ourselves and the other. Our love makes it easy to forgive the other person. We see our mate's good points and appreciate them. As much as possible, our love is unconditional.

If we are exceptionally mature and have a great deal of love, we can figure out a way to make any relationship work. Those are two big "ifs" and when they aren't satisfied, incompatibility becomes unhappiness.

So, relationships are naturally easier when we are compatible with our mate—when we see life in a similar way, approach challenges the same, or want to raise our children the same way. Some internet dating sites try to match people according to compatibility for this very reason. Some people search for their match for many years. Just remember, **people change.** We are growth-oriented beings, always evolving. Life events, new friends, different jobs, stressful situations can all influence the direction of our evolution. For two people to stay together over many years, they must communicate constantly throughout those changes, as well as being mature and loving.

We are not static, and as such, sometimes we change and discover that a relationship that was once happy and pleasant is no longer that way. We are not the same people, and where there once was compatibility, kindness and understanding, there is now much less. If both of us cannot act with consideration and maturity to rekindle our love, then the relationship is in trouble. It need not be seen as a failure however; change is a principle of the universe, like gravity, and sometimes the legs of a relationship become old and weak, so it falls down.

Keep clear lines of communication open to keep your partnership strong. Discuss things that are on your mind—deep things, not just practical household things. Think about how to be exceptionally mature and have a great deal of love. Keep tabs on your own attitude constantly, and most of all, appreciate your mate for who they are.

My Lover, My Mirror

When you point at someone,
three fingers point back at you.

I wonder how my life would be different if, when I was younger, I had been able to see my boyfriends more clearly. I truly believe if you pay attention, people will show you who they are. They'll say things that reveal their true nature; for example, a guy who enjoys putting down his friends has an unkind streak. Most of us are not very good listeners, and we spend so much time wrapped up in ourselves, we don't see what is really going on around us.

The time to pay attention is when you first meet someone. Once you are in a relationship, even a friendship, things get much more complicated. You start co-creating with that person, and what you are doing becomes intertwined with what the other person is doing. You'll feed off each other's good vibes as well as spiral downwards together.

When you first meet someone, you get to decide if his/her character matches the good points in yourself you'd like to bring out—if their personal trajectory is one you'd like to travel along side. There is so much variety in the world, and in our own vibration, we might meet someone when we're at a low point but if we're smart, we'll choose not to spend too much time with them. If you are having a bad day and manifest a car accident, you wouldn't automatically start dating the person that hit you, right? Our vibration averages over time, so if you're going through a few rough weeks, that's the time to be wary of starting a new relationship.

Once you're in an intimate relationship

(or long-time roommates or close friends), the other person really becomes your mirror. What annoys you most about them is a hot-point in your own life. What you get mad at them about, you're really mad at yourself about, in some aspect. Also remember the flip side of the golden rule. What you do to them, you are doing to yourself, and what they do to you, they are doing to themselves.

So, if you fight about how messy the house is, the solution is to **work together** on keeping the house cleaner, and being understanding when it isn't quite up to the standard you are looking for. When one is upset about how the other works too much, the solution is to **work together** to spend quality time together whenever possible and really make the time together count, or come up with another solution.

There is usually an issue inside the issue, and it's probably your issue if you're the one who is upset. Own your part of it, and realize that when you're intimately together, your issues link up too, and you'll need to work together to solve problems rather than putting it all onto one person. There is no *one person* anymore; you are co-creating your life together.

Contagious Vibrations

"It is possible for us to catch fear from others as much as we would catch a cold, for we are all unconscious mental, emotional and spiritual broadcasting stations." - Ernest Holmes

I noticed it first in our alpacas. Our baby alpaca, Allie, from one day old, seemed to be watching what the other alpacas were doing. She would watch them graze, and then she would imitate grazing even though she had no teeth and could not tear the grass off nor chew it. When she saw her big sisters laying in a small dirt patch—alpacas love dirt baths— she did it, too. It seemed quite clear to me that she was watching the others to learn how to be an alpaca. It's likely that many other herding animals do this as well.

It made me wonder—is this something people do? So, I started watching people to see how they interacted with those around them. From what I've seen, people do this *a lot*. Children watch their older siblings to see how they interact with their parents, and to see what they can get away with. They watch other children to learn playground rules, how to treat others, and probably a hundred other things that are too subtle for an outside observer to notice. This wasn't all that surprising—they are our young, and so they need to "learn how to be people." I was more surprised when I started noticing that adults do this a lot, too.

When one person holds the door for another, others following behind do the same. A rowdy person in a pub gives others permission to follow suit. When meeting someone new, we gauge a thousand parameters in the first few seconds—from their tone of voice and body language—and we respond accordingly. We read one another's mood, and respond in kind. If our grandma seems a little tired today, we tone it down a notch, don't we? We don't bowl her over with exciting news and hyperactive energy; we instinctively dial it down to match her energy. In crowds, in small groups, in pairs even—we take our cues from others around us on how to act. We do it most when we're in new or unfamiliar situations. By far, most of us will stick to the middle of the curve and not do anything too out of the ordinary in a group setting.

I believe we're using a combination of visual and auditory clues as well as energetic ones. It would be interesting to put ear plugs and a blindfold on someone and take them to a mall, grocery store or other public place and see what they can tell from energy alone.

This watching-others strategy comes from our tribal beginnings, and is likely necessary for the smooth functioning of a village. It helps us act in harmony with those around us. It seems to be an ability that all are born with to some degree, but some people, like myself, have a stronger gift of this sense. I instantly, unconsciously, adjust my speaking tone, style and vocabulary to match whom I'm speaking to. I even change my body language. When I learned to really pay attention to how I was feeling, I realized that I can even feel how people want to be treated.

I can tell when someone is deeply unhappy with themselves; they send out a rather ugly vibe that says "mistreat me." I can tell when someone feels good about themselves; they send out a vibe that says "respect me." I can tell when someone is stressed and frazzled; their vibe says "throw a wrench in my plans. It's what I'm used to."

This leads to the big idea for this chapter: **we show others how to treat us.** We do this using three forms: energetically, with body language, and lastly, words. Our vibration clearly broadcasts our intention of how we'd like to be treated. You may argue that no one **wants** to be mistreated, but their vibe says otherwise. A better way to say it is they *expect* to be mistreated, and so to make their dream (of being mistreated) come true, they ask everyone around them to do it.

It takes great integrity and awareness to treat someone kindly when they are sending out this "mistreat me" vibe. I learned this when I was a volunteer at a Victim Support Unit (VSU). Our clients were all deep in victim mentalities, and they really did not expect anything to go well. That intention manifested in our office as challenges with keeping the files organized, reaching people on the phone, or connecting clients with services they needed. They often expected to be hurt again, so VSU workers, police officers or lawyers would sometimes say the wrong things. Even with good intentions, we had difficulties because the client's intention (to be hurt again or for things to go badly) was so much stronger than ours. To be a good VSU worker, I realized, I had to set a very strong intention to be as helpful as possible and for things to go smoothly. My intention had to be as strong or stronger than the victim's.

This principle applies to anyone you are trying to help. You can't allow yourself to be pulled down to their level. You must maintain the highest, clearest image in your mind of their healthiest, happiest self—your intention must prevail. It is easy to learn this principle but harder to practice it.

~

One summer, a dear friend's world was shattered when one of her close friends committed murder. She was devastated. It was a complete shock. No one knew he had been that mentally ill. He had been like a brother to her, and she couldn't believe what he had done. The murder was in the headlines for days as the story unfolded and she dropped into deep despair.

Her own mental health was shattered. She was on the brink of losing her mind and taking her own life. I went over to her place many times and talked with her. She needed to feel there was some hope. We came up with a mantra that would help her to keep an even keel when she felt herself slipping into the oblivion of desperation. I realized that my challenge was to keep a vision of her as a whole, thriving, amazing, healthy woman in the front of my mind. I refused to see anything else, and would not join her in despair, although many times I was tempted to.

She gradually improved. She learned coping mechanisms and the trauma of the incident faded somewhat. I'm amazed that through it all, she never stopped loving her friend, although she could not understand what snapped in his mind. She called him regularly and even went to visit when she was allowed to. In time, she was the thriving, whole woman I envisioned; I'm so glad I never lost sight of who she truly is.

~

It would be nice if our vibrational message was as easy to read as a billboard. Often, we don't realize what kind of vibe we are broadcasting. We might be sending out a victim-like vibe—saying "hurt me," for example—without realizing it. We can look at the daily events in our lives for clues. How do people treat you, in general? What kinds of "random" events happen to you? Are they happy or upsetting?

To change the vibrational message you are sending out takes a clear desire to change, a new focus and strong intention. More on this in the next chapter.

Togetherness

We teach others how to treat us. We send out body language signals, subtle and obvious, and we send out vibrations that others pick up in that mystical, mysterious way and that attracts the experiences we are expecting.

Teresa Griffith

Having New Experiences

If you've read Tiny Book 2, *Intelligence is Everywhere—Looking at Animals, Vegetables, and Minerals,* you may remember learning about the non-physical dimensions of thought, imagination, and intention. To have new, different experiences with others, you have to have new thoughts, to put your imagination to work in new ways, and forge new intentions.

Let's look at a scenario. Suppose you have to go to the bank. You probably remember the last time you went and without realizing it, you'll replay the "mind movie" of the interactions with the clerks, so you'll create an intention to have more of the same. If it was particularly memorable—one of the clerks was rude to you or they wouldn't let you withdraw the money you needed—your imagination will be very active. To have a new style of interaction, you have to get your imagination to work on envisioning something new—a fun, pleasant interaction, instead of an angry one.

It can be surprisingly hard to set a new intention when you are so used to what you've been doing for a while. Your brain circuitry is wired for your usual way of being, and it takes a conscious effort to wire a new circuit. Brain and behaviour expert Dr. Joe Dispenza gives us hope, however. He says that you only have to repeat a new action or thought *once* to begin strengthening the new neural circuits and weakening the old ones.

The problem is that we are so used to the old circuits, it is easier to keep using them. Neurons that fire together, wire together, Dr. Joe says, and ones that fire together often get wired together strongly. We can still make new pathways, however, and learn new behaviours if we just choose the new way consistently.

Scientists have been learning so much about our neural activity and the patterns they see in unhealthy people. They can map the brain activity in Alzheimer's patients—the maps resemble swiss cheese—and then remap it after behavioural treatment to see the improvement. There is more hope than ever for these and other patients!

I tell you this to encourage you; if someone with a serious disease or injury can relearn how to do things, there is hope for you! If you are trying to learn to be more loving, more accepting, or make any sort of new neural pathways—it may be awkward at first, but you can do it. It is possible! Be easy about it.

Pay attention to how you feel. When you feel bad—fearful, angry, upset, sad, or any other bad-feeling emotion—your intuition or higher self is trying to remind you that you are not in harmony with the universe. Something you've been thinking about is small-minded, backwards-thinking, not growth-oriented, critical of others, or other thoughts that are harmful to your health. Steer your thoughts toward something that feels better.

Don't forget the power of the imagination. Don't let yourself replay the old movies. Stop yourself *every time* and set a new intention. When you have set the new intention, immediately try to imagine a new interaction in this relationship. Practice with easier things—like going to the grocery store— and when you get good at those, apply this new ability to the harder things in life.

Teresa Griffith

An Ocean of Differences

I once worked in an office that had an odd-man-out. That is, there was one man who worked there that almost everybody disliked. Let's call him V. My coworkers told me they didn't like V because he was rude and condescending to customers.

I decided early on that I would form my own opinion of V. I knew that everyone has their own experiences, and I shouldn't expect to have exactly the same issues with V. I found him to be generally okay, although there were times when I could tell he was stressed and hurried. He was abrupt with our customers at those times, even rude. Other days, he seemed fine to me. I decided to take him on a daily basis, rather than assuming the worst and feeling anxious when I realized I had to work with him.

In forming my own opinion of V, I also saw many of his good traits. He was very thorough in his work. He was confident and really knew the intricacies of the job. He was noticeably different from most of the other people in the office. He didn't look different— he wasn't a visible minority—but he acted very differently. He didn't chat with others during the slow times or join in on discussions about our local sports team's wins and losses. I'm fairly sure he kept to himself because he knew people talked about him behind his back. Some of my coworkers seemed to get a big thrill—a false sense of intimacy, I learned later—from alienating him and making him their common enemy. He probably also kept to himself because he felt different, because he was.

It can be challenging working or interacting with people who seem very different. Since we see the world through our particular lens, our viewpoint, it can be hard to understand someone else when their viewpoint is so different. Many factors contribute to our outlook in life, such as messages from our parents, beliefs held by the society we grew up in, things we learned in school—in the classroom and the playground —and beliefs we picked up from our life experiences. When people come from a vastly different part of the world, culture, or experiences, they pick up different/other messages and see the world in a very different way.

The differences can be subtle or huge. When I went to Cambodia recently, I was thinking about all four hundred of us packed into that airplane for the fourteen-hour flight. We came from every corner of the world, from every belief system and, presumably, religion. Yet here we were, having this experience together. It was peaceful and pleasant. We knew how to behave and we followed the rules

—only one man did not. At the end of the flight, the father of the family seated one row in front of me started loudly criticizing his son as they packed up their things. We were all tired of being cooped up, and this man just couldn't contain himself. I was surprised how much it bothered me that he broke the unspoken rule of air travel: he raised his voice!

Our society has a lot of unspoken rules and we instinctively expect everyone to follow them. When someone doesn't, we feel rattled. People from another culture don't always know the unspoken rules. They have their own set of cultural norms, which we may find uncomfortable or even alarming. Their "bad" behaviour touches a sore spot in us. It activates a piece of our shadow and we lash out (or we want to). Many times, we're not aware of our shadow, so we act unconsciously. Becoming conscious of all our motivations— shadow and light—helps us process the current situation and choose a course of action that doesn't inflame a situation. We can choose to disengage from the anger. We become peacemakers.

~

I looked up the Virtues card (see virtuesproject.org) for Peacefulness, and I feel like it was written by a group of people. There is such variety in the concepts that I don't think one person could have seen all those angles:

> *Peacefulness is inner calm and tranquility. It is a sense of harmony with all creation. Inner peace comes from quiet reflection and prayer. We release the past and let anxiety go. We keep a graceful pace, not allowing ourselves to be rushed or overwhelmed. We do not give in to anger. We resolve conflict in a just and gentle way. Peace is giving up*

the love of power for the power of love.
We choose the unity of peace over the
fragmentation of fear. Peace in the
world begins with peace in our lives.

Isn't that description great? The writers of this Virtues card covered some aspects I never would have thought of.

I often have to remind myself that not everyone thinks like me. Even my own family members, like my sisters, don't think like me, although we are about as similar as people can be.

People from different cultures, religions and belief systems can seem so different, we have difficulty relating. In Cambodia, I was amazed at their fascination with snakes. Snakes showed up in statues and murals everywhere. My tour-guide-extraordinaire explained the myth of a snake keeping Buddha afloat. So their love of snakes goes far deeper than I thought. They worship snakes, in a sense—although the word "worship" means something different in Cambodia, too.

Cambodian society, properly called Khmer, is a unique one nestled between the Vietnamese, Thai, Chinese and Laotian. Their religion is different, their food is different, their culture is different, and their climate is different. Their unspoken rules are different too; even on the hottest days, they do not wear tank tops or shorts, for example, because of a prevailing sense of modesty. This rule is actually spoken of plenty if you want to go to a holy place or visit the ruins at Angkor Wat.

On my last day there, I was walking by myself on a long promenade along the river. It was paved with stone slabs and went on for miles. I was striding along in my usual gait, confidently out to explore the world when I walked through a puddle. My left foot went out from under me and in classic cartoon style, legs and arms flailing, I slipped and landed on my hip in the puddle. A few men I had just nodded to came to my aid immediately, laughing somewhat, and offered me a hand to help me up. I was laughing too! And I was grateful for their help.

If you consider that everyone has their own perspective, then there are billions of different perspectives on this world. Yet, most would happily help you up out of a puddle. We are different yet the same.

At times, it feels like there is an ocean of different beliefs between us. Yet somehow we must learn how to live together on this planet. Conflicts break out because those differences seem too big to bridge sometimes. But wherever the conflicts are, there are those who believe in and are working towards harmony and peace. Look for those people. Join them!

Freeflow Giving

In all my years on the planet, in marriages, friendships, family relationships and teams, I have come to realize one big thing: my love is not a commodity to be budgeted, hoarded, or given out in measured portions. It comes from an infinite source—God—so there is no need to hold back. I do myself and everyone I meet—all of humanity, ultimately—a disservice when I treat love, kindness, compassion, and my attention as material things.

When I look at the world through the lens of materialism, I think that my relationships are things to be managed. They should be analyzed, optimized and profitable. I have caught myself thinking, why give my love to someone who does not reciprocate equally?

Shouldn't I focus my efforts on those who (appear to) love me as much as I love them? This, as you might know by now, is a very small idea. Besides, how do I really know who loves me equally?

Relationships are gifts. Every person I'm in relationship with deserves to be appreciated.

Why wouldn't I give all my gifts freely to my friends, family and spouse?

~

Love, compassion and even the gift of my attention are not to be withheld. It is so lovely to spend a moment giving my *full attention* to my sweet brown dog, Bunner. Why not give Jenny, our big black collie, the chance to lean on me and get rubbed behind the ears? I love going to see what the alpacas are doing. Since I visit them so often, they are very comfortable with me. It's so lovely to give them my attention—to observe them in the moment, fully present. The reward for doing so is the occasional close-up sniff by one of them, or another subtle gesture which seems to say, "I know you. You're the one who takes care of us. Thanks!"

There is no need, however, to do things for the reward. **Life itself is the reward!** Showing love to get a payout of love is just the tip of the love-iceberg; true love is deeper, and unconditional. Giving out love freely is the most natural thing in the world when you realize love is *unlimited.* And since when is it

If life itself is the reward, we've already been rewarded (since we have life). What is the reward for? Does there have to be a reason? We have done nothing to earn it —we are here by Universal grace and the nature of Source to want to explore itself.

We *have* the trophy; so why not stop striving and competing?

my job to decide who gets blessed? Since never. So, I can bless everyone I meet with my presence, my attention, and my love.

How does this look in a marriage? Since I am blessed to have a husband who thinks the same way I do about love, we don't play love-withholding games. We just love each other freely, all the time, and any lulls in the expression of love are short-lived ones caused by moments of exhaustion or hunger-induced grumpiness. We don't force each other not to love anyone else; we are free to love friends, family members, and even those intriguing individuals we feel an uncanny connection with. There is no limit to our love. There is no jealousy. To me, jealousy is an unspoken feeling of, "don't give that person the love that's owed to me!" Love is not a commodity to be bought, sold, lent or owed. It's a deep caring. It's me wanting what's best for you.

Sometimes I can't help but look at a stranger like a curious alpaca does, saying "who are you? You are interesting! Aren't you a neat God-child! Let's talk!" Since there is no jealousy and my husband and I don't have the slightest feeling of owning each other, I am free to talk to anyone, to form new friendships.

How does this kind of love look in friendship? This means there is no measuring of love-given and love-received. This includes time, favours, help or material gifts given. It means I would do anything for my friends. Occasionally, a friend doesn't reciprocate and although it's a little jarring, I must remind myself it's okay—it's not about equal exchanges. It's about giving freely. I love my friends, and I love supporting them unconditionally. I'll help in any way I can, and I do my very best not to keep track of who has done what.

This is counter-culture, isn't it? A very common message in North American culture is "take care of yourself first." It is even justified by a belief that you *can't* take care of anyone else *unless* you take care of yourself first. I think the intention is a good one—it's meant to prevent burnout—but it is taken to the extreme and abused. Some take this to mean that they don't need to take care of anyone else, ever. Some put themselves first *always,* and in so doing, miss out on the immense joy of serving others. Some might even justify narcissistic behaviour with the "take care of yourself first" motto. I don't object to taking care of yourself at all, but the word "first" seems to apply day or night, at all times. Taking care of yourself first can become a never-ending quest. Whenever we do something *first*, other things get pushed off to the side. Life is more fulfilling when we don't push others off to the side.

Mindlessly taking care of ourselves first, as if it were a command or iron-clad rule, shuts us down to opportunities and reinforces the idea that our time, love and resources are limited.

I have news for you. They aren't. Your love and attention are *completely unlimited.* Your physical resources have *barely any limits* on them—far fewer than you think. As for your time, the only moment that matters is *now.* Time spent with a friend is never wasted and should not be regretted.

I wonder if we could truly live by the counter-culture motto **take care of others first.** Has anyone ever done this? Mother Teresa might have been one. Is it realistic to live this way? Why not!? Try it. If I did it even eighty percent of the time, I can't imagine being happier or more fulfilled. Would I have unmet needs? Maybe, but would I be unhappy because of them? Would I even notice? The focus on having one's needs met is a recent one. It only started in the 1980's—before that, people didn't worry about their needs very much. I find it easy to dismiss that mental construct as a silly part of that "material girl" decade. When I remember that my time, love and attention are unlimited, I forget to be concerned about my needs. **When I remember that *Source* fills my needs, always, I can relax about them.**

This is huge: I stop worrying about someone else meeting my needs when I just give to those around me, in the flow of life, as I am able, and as the opportunities arise. When I used to focus on having my needs met, I first had to identify the unmet needs and then attempt to communicate them clearly to my husband/friend/parent—and talking about my needs always amplified the feeling of dissatisfaction in my life. **The expectation was that someone else could and would fulfill my need. When they couldn't or wouldn't, my expectations were dashed, and I felt hurt and unloved.** When I focus on giving to others—of my time, resources and *most importantly, my love*—in that amazing, freeflow way that works naturally and obviously, I am happy and my fundamental need for human connection is completely satisfied. With that need met, others are not an issue, and I feel happy, helpful, useful, and see the world as a friendly community.

~

Freeflow giving isn't contrived or condescending; it would never say "I need to give $100 to charity this month. Where should I spend it?" or "my friend Judy is such a mess. I should offer to babysit more so she can train for a better job." It happens in the flow of life,

Although I feel like I've discovered the principle "take care of others first," it is the same as that eternal message to "love your neighbour," perhaps with a little more action implied. From now on, however, I'll drop the word "first" to avoid a never-ending quest.

as situations occur and we see an opportunity to give.

All this talk of giving wasn't learned from a text book or pure inspiration from a meditation session—it was a real life lesson. We once helped a friend move and then let him live with us for nearly a year. We had been given the use of the UHAUL moving truck for several additional days, so we offered it to him. We were so glad to help; he had few prospects for his business and was quite unhappy where he had been living. Initially after moving, he found some new work and was generally doing well. He lived in the spare room and we enjoyed having him around. He helped out with yard and farm work when he wasn't running his business. After a while, he started feeling sorry for himself and was less helpful. We covered more and more of his expenses as he waited to be paid for work done. He was reluctant to "bother" the people who owed him money, however. So, he borrowed from us again and again and we happily helped.

Gradually, we realized we weren't as happy helping him. We wanted to be, but something didn't feel right. His attitude of self-pity was deeply entrenched, and we had a hard time understanding why. He decided to give up on his business, so we encouraged him and tried to help him see that he had skills and was too young to retire. It finally struck me one day—we were happy to help when he needed it, but he didn't really need it any more. That's why we were no longer happy about helping. He could get a job any time. So it was time for him to get one (and move out).

I wish I could say it ended in absolute peace and we're still friends, but before long, he stopped returning our calls. I think he felt bad about the money he owed us. So, we lost a friend over too much helping, but we still don't regret it. We learned what overhelping was, and the experience helped me form the idea of freeflow giving.

Freeflow giving is spontaneous and fun. It's not forced or filled with obligation or guilt. It's simply giving when you see a need you can fill, happily. Sometimes, it's just a smile or a word of encouragement.

One Saturday on our way out for breakfast, we were approached by an elderly lady who asked if we were going to the library. We said no, but would she like a hand getting there? She was using a walker to help her get around, but her real concern was the elevator. She asked if we would ride it with her, in case it stopped on the way up. Of course we would. She was so happy, but was planning to walk around outside for a little before going to the library—could we meet up with her in a little while? We agreed, telling her that she could find us in the nearby restaurant when she was ready to go up. She said she might go for breakfast too, so she would meet us there.

Our afternoon unfolded as I sat with her

while she finished breakfast; I spent a great deal of time listening to her talk. She was lonely, and she didn't even try to hide it. She told me her life story, more or less, and it was interesting to hear her talk about the hurts in her life from many years ago as if they had happened last week. She acknowledged that she was living in the past, but didn't know how to stop. I listened and listened, and only after a long time did I tell her that I thought she was doing extremely well, and that I could see she was capable of healing and living vibrantly. I encouraged her to go to her senior's group whenever possible—surely, she wasn't the only one who was lonely.

I'm so glad we didn't write her off as an old kook and avoid her. I enjoyed the time we spent getting to know her. The best part was encouraging her and showing her that someone cared. After a few hours, we made our way to the library elevator, only to find it was not even working!

~

Freeflow giving would be one helluva thing to go viral. Can you imagine what the world would look like? That's the kind of reality I want to live in, and so that's what I'm focusing on and spreading around as much as possible!

Focusing on contributing changes the way you interact with the world. Rather than just working for a paycheque, I often think of how I am helping those at work. They need my expertise. When I am tired or grumpy, I remind myself that my clients and coworkers need me to be professional and pleasant, not selfish and hurried. I am contributing to the world I work in by providing good service. The *contribution* is the motivation, instead of just putting in my time to get money to spend on my days off.

Freeflow giving gets us out of our little,

inward-turned world. It helps us see that we have a place in the larger world, and fills our fundamental need for human connection.

Practice loving without limits, appreciating everyone. Grab hold of the *take care of others* vision and make it reality, one small act at a time, as the freeflow giving opportunities arise.

Togetherness

About the Author

Teresa Griffith draws inspiration from nature and shares stories from her life on a small farm in Canada. She has also written *Love Your Skeletons,* a guide to overcoming painful or embarrassing skeletons in your closet, and *York Boat Captain -- 18 Life-Changing Days on the Peace River.*

In her series of Tiny Books on Big Ideas, she shares revolutionary principles and observations of how the universe works, the roots of happiness, connecting with profound intelligence, and deep, inspired wisdom on relationships with others and ourselves.

For more information or to contact Teresa, visit teresagriffith.ca.

Togetherness

www.ingramcontent.com/pod-product-compliance
Lightning Source LLC
LaVergne TN
LVHW021549080426
835510LV00019B/2448